T0194961

Foundation

OF THE
CHRISTIAN FAITH

LARRY COLLINS

WESTBOW
PRESS®
A DIVISION OF THOMAS NELSON
& ZONDERVAN

WestBow Press books may be ordered through booksellers or by contacting:

WestBow Press
A Division of Thomas Nelson & Zondervan
1663 Liberty Drive
Bloomington, IN 47403
www.westbowpress.com
1 (866) 928-1240

ISBN: 978-1-9736-8219-6 (sc)
ISBN: 978-1-9736-8218-9 (e)

Print information available on the last page.

WestBow Press rev. date: 12/12/2019

here is places the Bible that compares the life of a believer to the construction of a building or an edifice. For instance, in the epistle of Jude, verse 20, we read, but you beloved, building yourselves up on your most holy faith, praying in the holy spirit. The apostle Paul also uses the same picture in 1 Cor.3: 9,10, he says, for we are God's fellow workers, you are God's field, you are building. V-10, According to the grace of God, which was given to me, as a wise master builder I have laid the foundation, and * another builds on it. But let each one take heed how he builds on it. Eph. 2:22, he says, in whom you also are being built together for a dwelling place of God in the spirit. Col. 2:7, It says, rooted and built up in him and stablished in the faith, as you have been taught, abounding in it with thanksgiving. In acts, 20:32, Paul speaking to the elders of the church at Ephesus, he says, So now brethren, I commend you to God and to the word of his grace, which is able to build you up and give you an inheritance among all those who are sanctified. In all these passages, the believer's life is compared to the construction of a building.

Now, in the natural order, the first and most important feature of any solid and permanent building is the foundation. The foundation sets a limit to the weight and height of the building which is to be erected upon it. A weak foundation can only support a small building. A strong foundation can support a large building. There is a fixed relationship between the foundations and the building.

Even so in the spiritual order, the same thing happens in the lives of many professing Christians. The set out with every intention of raising a fine building of Christianity in their lives. But alas, before long, their fine building begins to sink to sag, to get out of true. Sometimes it even collapses completely, and leaves nothing but a ruined heap of vows and prayers and good intentions which have done unfulfilled.

Beneath the mass of ruins, the reason for the failure lies buried. It was the foundation, which was never properly laid, and which was unable to support the fine building which it was proposed to erect. What, then, is God's appointed foundation for the Christian life?

The answer is clearly given by the Apostle Paul in first Corinthians 3:11, For no other foundation can any 0ne lay than that which is laid, which is Christ Jesus. This is also confirmed by the Apostle Peter. First Peter 2:6, where Peter speaks of Jesus Christ, and says, wherefore also it is contained in the scripture, behold, I lay in Zion a chief corner stone, elect, precious, and he who believes on him will by no means be put to shame. The scripture to which Peter here refers is found in Isaiah 28:16, where it says, Therefore, thus says the Lord God, Behold, I lay in Zion a stone for a Foundation, a tried stone, a precious cornerstone, a sure foundation; whoever believes will not act hastily.

The old testament and new testament a like agree in this fact, the true foundation of the Christian Life is Jesus Christ himself, nothing else, and no one else. IT is not a creed, not a church, not a denomination, not an ordinance or ceremony. It is Jesus Christ himself. 1 Cor. 3: 11, For no other foundation can anyone lay than that which is laid, which is Jesus Christ.

In this connection it is helpful also to consider the words of Jesus himself. In Matthew's Gospel, we read the following conversation between Jesus and his disciples. Matt. 16: 13-18, When Jesus came into the region of Caesarea Philippi, he asked his disciples, saying, whom do men say that I the son of man am? V-14, so they said, some say John the

Baptist, some Elijah and others Jeremiah, or one of the prophets. V-15, He said to them, but who do you say that I am? V-16, And Simon Peter answered and said, you are the Christ, the son of the living God. V-17, Jesus, answered and said to him, blessed are you, Simon Bar-Jonah, for flesh and blood has, not revealed this to you, but my father who is in heaven. V-18 And I also say to you, that you are Peter, and upon this rock I will build my church, and the gates of hades shall not prevail against it.

Now it has sometimes been suggested that these words of Jesus mean that the Apostle Peter is the rock upon which the Christian Church is to be built, and that Peter is in some sense the foundation of Christ himself. This question of the true foundation is such vital and far reaching importance that it is desirable to examine the words of Jesus very carefully, in order to make sure of their proper meaning.

In the original Greek of the New Testament there is, in the answer of Christ to Peter, a deliberate play upon words. In Greek, the name Peter is (Petros), the word for rock is (Petra). Playing upon this similarity in sound, Jesus says, in Matt. 16: 18, You are Peter (Petros), and on this rock (Petra), I will build my church.

Though there is a similarity in sound between these two words, their meaning is quite different. Petros means a small stone or pebble, Petra means a large rock, the idea of building a church upon a pebble would obviously be ridiculous, and therefore could not be Christ's real meaning.

There is one modern language in which it is possible, even in translation, to retain something of this play upon words. That language is French. The French form of the name Peter is (Pierre). In French Pierre also means a stone on the other hand, the French word for rock is (Rocher). Thus, in the French version of the New Testament, Jesus says to Peter, in Matt. 16:18, You are Peter (Pierre, a stone), and upon this rock, (Rocher), I will build my church.

In this way, the French version brings out the same point as the original Greek. Jesus is not identifying Peter with the rock, on the contrary. He is contrasting Peter with the rock. He is pointing out how small and insignificant the little stone, Peter, is to comparison to the great rock upon which the church is to be built. The church to be built upon the plane that Peter was in when God Revealed to him who Jesus was, (The Spirit, Holy Spirit) Christ Himself.

Common sense and scripture alike confirm this fact. If the church of Christ was really founded upon the Apostle Peter, it would have been the insecure and unstable edifice in the world. Just a little further on in Matthew,16:22,23, we read that Jesus began to forewarn his disciples of his impending rejection and crucifixion.

Matt. 16: 22,23,Then Peter took him aside and begun to rebuke him saying, for be it from you, Lord; This shall not happing to you, v-23, But he (Christ) turned and said to Peter, " Get thee behind me, Satan, you are an offence to me, for you are not mindful of the thing of God, but the thing of men."

Here Christ, directly charges Peter with being influenced in his thinking by the opinions of men and even by the promptings of Satan himself. How could such a man be the foundation of the entire Christian Church?

Late, in the gospels, we read that rather than confess Christ before a serving maid, Peter publicly denied his lord three times.

Even after the resurrection and the day of Pentecost, Paul tells us, in Galatians, Chapter 2, Versus 11 to 14, that Peter was influenced by fear of his countryman to compromise at the point concerning the truth of the gospel.

Surely then, Peter was no rock, he was loveable, impetuous but a man just like the rest, with all the inherent weakness and failings of humanity. The only rock upon which true and stable Christian faith can be based is Christ himself. Plan confirmation of this fact concerning the foundation of all true scriptural faith is found also in the old testament.

In Psalm 18:2, the Psalmist David, prophetically inspired by the holy spirit, says this, the lord is my rock and my fortress and my deliverer; my God, my strength, in whom I will trust; my shield and the horn of my salvation, and my stronghold.

David again makes a smaller confession of faith in Psalm 62: 1,2, saying, truly my soul silently waits for God, from him comes my salvation. V-2, He only is my rock and my salvation, he is my defense, I shall not be greatly moved. Again, in Psalm 62:5-7, David says, my soul, wait silently for God alone, for my expectation is from him. V-6, He only is my rock and my salvation, he is my defense, I shall not be moved. V-7, In God is my salvation and my glory, the rock of my strength, and my refuge, is in God.

Nothing could be plainer that that. Notice the empathic repetition of the word (only), which occurs five time. That is to say, the work rock and the word salvation are by the scripture intimately and inseparably joined. Each is found only in one person and that person is the lord himself.

If anyone should require yet Further Confirmation of this, we may turn to the works of Peter himself. Speaking to the people of Israel concerning Jesus Christ of Nazareth, in Acts 4: 12, says, nor is there salvation in any other, for there is no other name under Heaven given among men, by which we must be saved.

The lord Jesus Christ, therefore, himself, alone is the true rock, the rock of ages, in who there is salvation. The person who builds upon this foundation can say, like David, In PSA. 62:2, He only is my rock and my salvation, he is my defense, I shall not be greatly moved. How then does a person begin to build upon this rock, which is Christ?

Let us turn back again to that dramatic moment when Christ and Peter stood face to face, and Peter said, in Matt. 16: 16, Thou art the Christ, the son of the living God. Let us see for ourselves exactly what transpired between them. We have seen that the rock is Christ himself. But it is not Christ in isolation or in abstraction. There was a definite personal experience on the part of Peter. We may analyze four successive strategies in this experience of Peter.

First, there was a direct, personal confrontation of Peter by Christ. Christ and Peter stood face to face. There was no mediator between them. No other human being played any part at all in the experience. Second, there was a direct, personal revelation granted to Peter. Jesus said to Peter, in Matt. 16: 17, For flesh and blood has no revealed this to you, but my father who is in heaven. This was not the outcome of natural reasoning or of intellectual understanding. It was the outcome of a direct spiritual revelation to Peter by God the father himself.

Third, there was a personal acknowledgement by Peter of the truth which had been revealed to him. Fourth, there was an open and public confession by Peter of the truth which he acknowledged.

In these four successive stages we see what it means to build upon the rock. There is nothing purely abstract, or intellectual, or theoretical, about the whole thing. In each stage, there is a definite individual experience.

The first stage is a direct, personal confirmation of Christ. The second stage is a direct, spiritual revelation of Christ. The third stage is a personal acknowledgement of Christ. The fourth stage is an open and personal confession of Christ.

It is Christ experienced, Christ revealed, Christ acknowledged and confessed, it is Christ who in this way becomes for each individual believer the rock upon which is faith is built.

The question arises, is such an experience possible today? Can a person today come to know Christ in the same direct and personal way that Peter came to know him then? To his important question we must answer yes, for the following reasons.

First it was not Christ in his purely human nature who was revealed to Peter, Peter already knew Jesus of Nazareth, the carpenter's son. The one who was now revealed to Peter the divine, eternal, unchanging son of God. This is the same Christ who now lives exalted in heaven at the father's right hand. In the passage of two thousand years there has been no changed in him at all. Heb. 13: 8, Jesus Christ is the same yesterday, today, forever. As he was revealed to Peter, he can still be revealed today to those who sincerely seeks him.

Second, the revelation did not come by flesh and blood it did not come by any physical or sensory means. It was a spiritual revelation, the word of God's own holy spirit. The same spirit who gave this revelation Peter is now at work in all the world, revealing the same Christ. Jesus himself promised his disciples in John 16:13-14, However, when he, the spirit of truth, has come, he will guide you into all truth; for he will not speak on his own authority, but whatever he hears he will speak; and he will tell you things to come. V-14, He will glorify me, for he will take of what is mine and declare it to you.

Since the entire revelation is in the eternal spiritual realm, t is not limited in any way by maternal or physical factors, such as the passage of time, or the change of language, or customs, or clothing, or circumstances.

This individual and personal experience of Jesus Christ the son of God by the Holy Spirit revealed, acknowledged, and confessed, remains the one true unchanging rock, the one unmovable foundation, upon which all true Christian faith must be based. Creeds and opinions, churches, and denominations all these may change, but this one true rock of God's salvation by personal faith in Christ remains eternal and unchanging. Upon it a person may build his faith forever and for eternity with a security and confidence which nothing can even overcome.

John 17:3, "And this is eternal life, that they may know you the only true God, and Jesus Christ, whom you have sent." This is not only to know God in a general way through nature or conscience, as creator or judge. This is to know God revealed personally in Jesus Christ, neither is it to know about Jesus Christ, as only a historical character of a great teacher. It is to know Christ himself, directly and personally, and God in him.

1 John 5:13, These things I have written to you who believe in the name of the son of God, that you may know that you have eternal life, and that you may continue to believe in the name of the son of God. The early Christians did believe, they also knew that they had faith which produced a definite knowledge of that which they believed.

1 John 5:20, And we know that the son of God, has come, and has given us an understanding that we may know him who is true, and we are in him who is true, in his son Jesus Christ. This is the true God and eternal life.

Note the humble, and confidence of these words. Their basis is knowledge of a person, and that person in Jesus Christ himself.

Th Apostol Paul gave the same kind of personal testimony in 2 Tim. 1:12, when he said, For this reason I also suffer these things; nevertheless I am not ashamed, for I know whom I have believed, and am persuaded that he is able to keep what I have committed to him until that day. Notice that Paul did not say, I know what I have believed. He said, I know who I have believed. His faith was not founded upon a creed or a church, but upon a person, whom he knew by direct acquaintance, and that person was Jesus Christ. He had confidence concerning the well of his soul, which nothing in time or eternity could overthrow.

Job 22:21, Now acquaint yourself with him, and be at peace, thereby good will come to you.

II. HOW TO BUILD ON THE FOUNDATION

The Bible Foundation of Faith, Proof of Discipleship, Test of Love, Means of Revelation

Once we have laid in our own lives the foundation of this personal encounter with Christ, in what way can we continue to build upon this foundation? Or, more briefly, how to build upon the foundation once laid?

The answer to this question is found in the well-known parable about the wise man and the foolish man. Each of who built a house related for us by Christ in Matthew 7:24-27.

Therefore, whosoever hears these saying of mine, and does them, I will liken him to a wise man, who built his house on the rock. V-25, and the rain descended, the floods came, and the winds blew and beat on that house, and it did not fall, for it was founded on the rock. V-26, But everyone who hears these sayings of mine, and does not do them will be like a foolish man, who built his house on the sand; V-27, and the rain descended, and the floods came and the winds blew, and beat on that house, and it fell and great was the fall . Notice carefully that the difference between these men did not lie in the tests to which their houses were subjected. Each man's house had to endure the storm, the wind, the rain, the floods, Christianity has never offered anyone a storm free passage to heaven.

We are warned in Acts 14: 22, we must through many *tribulation enter the kingdom of God. Any road sign posted to heaven, which by passes tribulation, is a deception. It will not lead to the promised destination.

What, then, was the real difference between the two men and their houses? The answer is that the wise man built upon a foundation of rock, the foolish man upon a foundation of sand. The wise man built in such a way that his house came through the storm unmoved and secure, the foolish man built in such a way that his house could not weather the storm.

Just what are we to understand by this picture of building upon a rock? Just what does it mean for each of us as Christians in plain, simple language? Christ himself make this very plain, for he says, in Matt. 7: 24, whoever hear these sayings of mine, and does them, I will liken him to a wise man, who built his house upon a rock. Thus, building upon the rock consists of Hearing and doing the words of Christ.

Once the foundation of Christ himself the rock, has been laid in our lives, we build upon that foundation by hearing and doing the word of God that is, by diligently studying and applying in our lives the teaching of God's word. It was for this reason that the apostle Paul said, to the elders of the church at Ephesus, Acts 20: 32, So now, brethren, I commend you to God, and to the word of his grace, which is able to build you up and give you an inheritance among all those who are sanctified. It is God's word, and God's word alone, as we hear it and do it, as we study it and apply it, which is able to build up within us believers, a strong, secure edifice of faith, laid upon the foundation of Christ himself.

The brings us to a subject of supreme importance in the Christian faith, the relationship between Christ and the Bible and the relationship of each Christian to the Bible.

Throughout its pages, the Bible declares itself to be the word of God. There are number of passages in the scriptures where the same title the word, or the word of God is given by Jesus Christ himself. For example, in John's gospel, John 1: 1, In the beginning was the word and the word was with God and the word was God. John 1:14, And the word become flesh, and dwelt among us, and we beheld his glory, the glory as of the only begotten of the father, full of grace and truth.

Again, in Revelation 19:13, he (Christ) was clothed with a robe dipped in blood, and his name is called the word of God.

This identity of name reveals an identity of nature. The Bible is the word of God and Christ is the word of God. Each is a divine, perfect revelation of God. Each agrees perfectly with the other. The Bible perfectly reveals Christ, Christ perfectly fulfils the Bible. The Bible is the written word of God, Christ is the living word of God. Before his incarnation, Christ was the eternal word with the father. In his incarnation Christ is the word made flesh. The same holy spirit that reveals God through his written word, the Bible, reveals God in the word made Flesh, as Jesus of Nazareth.

If Christ is the perfect one with the Bible, then the relationship of the believer to the Bible must be the same as his relationship to Christ. To this fact the scriptures bear testimony in the bible.

In the fourteenth chapter of John, Jesus is warning his disciples that he is about to be taken from them in bodily presence, and that there will be a new kind of relationship and fellowship between him and them. The disciples are unable and unwilling to accept or to understand this impending change. They are unable to understand how, if Christ is about to go away from them, they will still be able to see him or have communication with him after he has left them.

In John 14:19, Christ says, A little while longer, and the world will see me no more, but you will see me. Because I live, you will live also. Because of this statement by Jesus, Judas asks in John 14: 22, Judas (not Iscariot) lord, how is it that you will manifest yourself to us, and not to the world? In other words, lord, how is if you are going away, and if the world will see you no more, by what means will you still be able to manifest yourself to us, your disciples, but not to the world, what kind of communication will you be able to maintain with us?

In John 14: 23, Jesus answers this question and says," If anyone loves me, he will keep my words and my father will love him, and we will come to him, and make our home with him."

The key to proper understanding of this answer is found in the phrase in v-23, "He will keep my words." The main feature which distinguishes a true disciple from the people of the world is that a true disciple is one who keeps Christ's words. If we now relate Christ's answer here given to the original question, John 14:22, Lord, how will you manifest yourself to us, and not to the world? We find revealed in this answer four facts of importance for every person who sincerely desires to be a real Christian.

For the sake of absolute clarity, let me fist repeat the answerer of Jesus in John 14: 23. "If anyone loves me, he will keep my words; and my father will love him, and we will come to him and make our home with him.

Here are the four vital facts concerning God's word, which are revealed by Christs answer. First, the keeping of God's word is the distinguishing feature which marks out the disciple of Christ from the rest of the world. Second, the keeping of God's word is the supreme test of the disciple's love for the disciple. Third, it is through God's word, as it is kept and obeyed, that Christ manifests himself to the disciple. Fourth, it is through God's word that the father and the son together come into the life of the disciple and establish their enduring home with him.

Side by side with the answer of Christ, let us set the words of the apostle John in the first Epistle of first John 2:4-5, He who says, I know him, and does not keep his commandments, is a lair and the truth is not in him. V-5, But whoever keeps his word, truly is the love of God is perfected, in him by this we know we are in him.

We see from these two passages that it is almost impossible to overestimate, or overemphasize, the importance of the place of God's word in the life of the Christian believer.

Let me present these truths to you in a direct and personal way. The keeping of God's word is the supreme distinguishing feature which should mark you out from the world as a disciple of Christ. It is the test of your love for God. It is the cause of God's love and favor toward you. It is the way that Christ will manifest himself to you. It is the way that God the father and God the son will come into your life and make their home with you.

Let me put it to you in this way. Your attitude toward God's word is your attitude toward God himself. You do not love God more that you love his word. You do not obey God more than you obey his word.

You do not honor God more than you honor his word. You do not have more room in your heart and life for God that you have for his word.

Do you want to know how much God means to you? You can easily find out. Just ask yourself how much does God's word mean to me? The answer to the second question is the answer also to the first. God means as much to you as his word means to you, just that much, and no more.

There is today a general awareness among all sections of the Christian church that we have entered into the period of the time foretold in Acts 2:17. And it shall come to pass in the last days says God, that I will pour out my spirit on all flesh, your sons and your daughters shall prophesy, your young men shall see visions, your old men shall dream dreams.

I believe firmly in the scriptural manifestation in these days of all nine gifts of the holy spirit. I believe that God speaks to his believing people through prophecies, visions, dreams, and other forms of supernatural revelation. But I hold most firmly that the scriptures are the supreme, authority means by which above all others, God speaks to his people, reveals himself to his people, guides and directs his people. All other forms of revelation must be carefully proved by reference to the scriptures.

In 1Thess. 5:19-21, we are told, do not quench the spirit. V-20, Do not despise prophecies. V-21, Test all things, hold fast what is good.

It is wrong, therefore, to quench any genuine manifestation of the holy spirit. It is wrong to despise any prophecies given through the holy spirit. On the other hand, it is vitally necessary to prove to test, to check any manifest station of the spirit, or any prophecies, by reference to the standard of the scriptures, and to have the facts in accepting it, to retain only those manifestations or prophecies which are in full accord with this divine standard.

In Isaiah 8:20, we are told, to the law and to the testimony! If they do not speak according to this word, it is because there is no light in them. An alternative translation is, if they speak not according to this word, they are not his. The scripture, the word of God is the supreme standard by which all else must be judged and tested. No doctrine, no practice, no prophecy, no revelation is to be accepted if it is not in full accord with the word of God. In whatever respect or whatever degree any person, any group, any organization, or any church departs from the word of God, in that respect and in that degree, they are in darkness, there is no light in them they are not to be listen to.

The scriptures warn that side by side with the increased activity and manifestation of the holy spirit, there will be a parallel increase in the activity of the satanic and demonic forces which always seek to oppose and strive against God's people and God's purpose in the Earth.

Speaking about how close the end time is Christ himself warns us in Matt. 24:23-25, Then if any one shall say to you, look, here is Christ, or there, do not believe it, v-24, For false Christs, and false prophets, will rise and show great signs and wonders, to deceive if It were possible, even the elect. V-25, see I have told you beforehand.

Apostle Paul warns us in 1 Tim. 4:1-3, Now the spirit expressly says that in latter times some will depart from the faith, giving heed to deceiving spirits and doctrines of demons.

V-2, Speaking lies in hypocrisy, having their conscience seared with a hot iron, V-3, Forbidding to marry and commanding to abstain from foods, which God has created to be received with Thanksgiving by those who believe and know the truth. Paul here warns us that in these days there will be a great increase in the propaganda of false doctrines and cults, and that the unseen cause behind this will be the activity of demon spirits.

He mentions religious doctrines and practices which impose unnatural and unscriptural forms of asceticism regarding diet and to the normal marriage relationship. Paul indicates that the safeguard against being deceived by these forms of religious error is to believe and know the truth that is, the truth of God's word. By this divine standard of truth, we are enabled to detect and to reject all forms of satanic error and deception. But for people who profess religion, without sound faith and knowledge of what the scripture teaches, these are indeed perilous days.

We need to lay hold upon one great guiding principle which is established in the scripture. It is this, God's word and God's spirit should always work together in perfect unity and harmony. We should never divorce the word from the spirit, or the spirit from the word.

Psalm 33:6, by the word of the lord the heavens were made and all host of them by the breath of his mouth. The word here translated breath is the normal Hebrew word breath suggests spirit. However, the use of the word breath suggests a beautiful picture of the working of God's spirit. As God's word goes out of his mouth, so his spirit which is his breath goes with it. As God's word goes forth, his breath that is, his spirit goes with it. In this way, God's word and God's spirit are always together, perfectly united in one single divine operation.

We see this illustrated in the account of creation. Gen. 1:2 The earth was without form, and void; and darkness was on the face of the deep and the spirit of God was hovering over the face of the waters. V-3, Then God said, "let there be light", and there was light. God's word went forth. God pronounced the word light and as the word and spirit of God were united, creation took place, light came into being Gods purpose was fulfilled.

What was true of that great act of creation is also true in the life of individual. God's word and God's spirit united in our lives contain all the creative authority and power of God himself. Through them God will supply every need and will work out his perfect will and plan for us. But if we divorce these two from one another, seeking the spirit without the word, or studying the word without the spirit, we go astray and miss God's plan.

To seek the manifestations of the spirit without the word will always end in foolishness, and error. To profess the word without the quickening of the spirit results only in dead, powerless orthodoxy and religious formalism.

We build upon the foundation of Christ in our lives by hearing and doing the word of God. It is God's word which builds us up.

God's word is the test of our discipleship and of our love for God, it is the way by which Christ manifests himself to us, and by which God in his fulness comes to make his home with us.

As we move forward in the great last day outpouring of God's spirit, we need, more than ever before, to hold fast to God's word.

God's word and God's spirit united in our lives will accomplish God's perfect will for us.

III. THE AUTHORITY OF GOD'S WORD

The only foundation of all true Christian faith is none other than Christ himself, Christ encountered, Christ revealed, Christ Acknowledged, and Christ Confessed.

We build upon this foundation of Christ in our lives by hearing and doing the word of God, by studying and applying the Bible. It is the Bible that builds us up. It is through the Bible, the written word of God, that Christ himself, the living word, the word made flesh, comes into our lives. Our attitude to the Bible is the test or proof of our love for Christ. The way by which Christ reveals himself to us.

In John 10:34-36, Christ is speaking to the Jews, and he is justifying the claim which he has made, and which the Jews had contested, that he is the son of God. In support of his claim, Christ quotes from the book of Psalms in the old testament, which he designates by the phrase, you law. Here Is what he says, in John 10:34-36, Jesus answered them, "Is it not written in your law, I said you are gods? V-35, If he called them gods, to whom the word of God came, (and the scripture cannot be broken), V-36, Do you say of him, whom the father sanctified and sent into the world, you are blaspheming, because I said, I am the son of God?

In this reply Jesus himself makes use of two titles which have ever since been used more than all others by his followers to designate the Bible. The first of these titles is "The word of God," The second is the "scripture." It will be profitable to consider what each of these two main titles must tell us about the nature of the Bible. When Jesus called the Bible the word of God, he indicated that the truths revealed in it did not have their origin with men, but with God. Though many different men have been used in various ways to make the Bible available to the world, they are all were instruments of channels. In no case did the message or the revelation of the Bible originate with men, but always and only with God himself.

When Jesus used the second title the scripture, he indicated a divinely appointed limitation of the Bible. The phrase "the scripture" means that which is written. The Bible does not contain the entire knowledge or purpose of almighty God in every aspect or detail. IT does not even contain all the divine inspired messages that God has ever given through human instruments. This is proved by the fact that the Bible itself refers in many places to the utterances of prophets whose words are not recorded in the Bible, we see, therefore, that the Bible, though completely true and authoritative, is also highly selective. the message is intended primarily for human race. Its central theme and purpose of the spiritual welfare of man. It reveals primarily the nature and consequences of sin, and the way of deliverance from sin and its consequences through faith in Christ.

Jesus not only set his personal seal of approval upon the Bible's two main titles, the word of God and the scripture. He also sets his seal of approval quite clearly upon the Bible's claim to complete authority. In John 10: 35, he says, "and the scripture cannot be broken." This short phrase, for supreme and divine authority that can ever be made on behalf of the Bible. Volumes of controversy may be written either for or against the Bible, but in the last resort Jesus has said all that in necessary in five short, simple words.

When we give the proper weight to the Bible's claim that the men associated with it were in every case were instruments or channels, and that every message and revelation in it has its origin with God himself, there remains no logical or reasonable ground for rejecting the Bible's claim to complete authority. We are living in days when men can launch satellites into space and then by means of invisible forces such as radio, radar, or electronics, control the course of these satellites at distances of thousands of millions of miles, can maintain communication with them and can receive communication from them. If men can achieve such results as these, then only blind prejudice and that of a most unscientific character would deny the possibility that God could create human beings with mental and spiritual faculties such that he could control or direct them, maintain communication with them, and receive communication from them. The Bible asserts that this is in fact what God has done and continues to do. The discoveries and inventions of modern science, so far from discrediting the claims of the Bible, make it easier for honest and open-minded people to picture the kind of relationship between God and men which made the Bible possible.

The Bible indicates plainly that there was one scripture, invisible influence by which God did in fact control, direct and communicate with the spirits and minds of the men by whom the Bible was written. This invisible influence is the holy spirit, God's own spirit.

For example, in 2 Tim. 3:16, the apostle Paul says, all scripture is given by inspiration of God, and is profitable for doctrine, for reproof, for correction, for instruction in righteousness. The word here translated by inspiration means inbreathed of God, is directly connected with the word "spirit." In other words, the spirit of God, the holy spirit was invisible, but influence which controlled and directed all those who wrote the parts of the Bible.

This is stated perhaps more plainly by the Apostle Peter, in 2 Pet.1:20, He says, knowing this first, that no prophecy of scripture is of any private interruption. In other words, as we have already explained in the message or revelation of the Bible originate with man, but always with God.

Then Peter goes on to explain just how this took place. 2 Pet. 1: 21, For prophecy never came by the will of man, but holy men of God spoke as they were moved by the Holy Spirit. The Greek word here translated "moved by" means more literally "borne along by" or we might say directed in their course by. In other words, just as men today control the course of their satellites in space by the interplay of radio and electronics, so God controlled the men who wrote the Bible by the interplay of his divine spirit with the spiritual and mental faculties of man. In the face of contemporary scientific evidence, to deny the possibility of God doing this, is just to give expression to prejudice.

In the Old Testament the same truth of divine inspiration is presented to us in another picture taken from an activity in which goes much further back into human history than the contemporary launching of satellites into space. In Psalm 12:6, David says, the words of the lord are pure words, like silver tried in a furnace of earth, purified seven times. The picture is taken from the process of purifying silver in a furnace, or oven, built of clay. The application of this picture to the writing of the Bible is as follows. The clay furnace represents the human element. The silver represents the divine message which is to be conveyed through the human channel. The fire which ensures the absolute purity of the silver, that is, the absolute accuracy of the message, represents the holy spirit. The phrase seven times indicates as the number seven does in many passages of the Bible, the absolute perfection of the holy spirit's work. Thus, the whole picture assures us that the complete accuracy of the divine message in the scripture is due to the perfect operation of the holy spirit, overruling all the frailty of human clay, and purging all the chance of human error from them the flawless silver of God's message to man.

Probably no character in the old testament had a clearer understanding than the Psalmist David of the truth and authority of God's word. In Psalm 119:89, he says "Forever, O' lord, your word is settled in heaven." Here David emphasizes that the Bible is not the product of time, but of eternity. It contains the eternal mind and counsel of God formed before the beginning of time or the foundation of the world. Out of eternity it has been projected through channels into this world of time, but when time and the world shall have passed away, the mind and counsel of God revealed through the scriptures will still unmoved and unchanged. The same thought is expressed by Christ himself in Matt. 24:35, where he says, "Heaven and earth will pass away, but my words will by no means pass away."

Again, in Psalm 119:160, The entirety of your word is truth, and every one of your righteous judgments endures forever. In Genesis 1: 1, it say, In the beginning God *created the heavens and the earth. Therefore, when David said, in Psa. 119: 160, The entirely of your word is truth. He is specifically referring to the book of Genesis. In the last century or two, persistent criticism and attack have been directed against almost every part of the Bible, both Old and New Testaments. However, by far the greatest of this attack has always been focused on the book of Genesis and the next four books which follow it, that is, on the first five books of the Bible, known as the Pentateuch, and attributed to the authorship of Moses. It is remarkable, therefore, that nearly three thousand years before these attacks against the Pentateuch were conceived in the minds of men, David had already given the holy spirit's testimony to the faith of God's believing people throughout all ages. Psa. 119: 160, The entirety of your word is truth. In other words, the Bible is true from Genesis 1:1 right on through Revelation 22: 21.

Certainly, if we are willing to give words their plain and obvious meaning, there can be no question that Christ and his apostles, like all believing Jews of their time, accepted the absolute truth and authority of all the Old Testament scriptures, including the five books of the Pentateuch.

In the account of Christ's temptation by Satan in the wilderness, recorded in Matthew 4:1-10, we read that Christ answered each temptation of Satan by direct quotation from the Old Testament scriptures. Three times he commenced his answer with the phrase, Matt. 4: 4, 7, 10, "It is written." Each time he was quoting directly from the book of Deuteronomy. It is a remarkable fact that not only Christ, but also Satan, accepted the absolute authority of this book. In the sermon on the mount, Matt. 5:17-18, Christ said, "Do you think that I am come to destroy the law, or the prophets. I did not come to destroy, but to fulfil. V-18, For assuredly I say to you, till heaven and earth pass away, one jot or one tittle will by no means pass from the law till all is fulfilled." The phrase "The law" was used to designate primarily the five books of Moses. That is, the Pentateuch, but also by extension, the rest of the Old Testament.

The word "got" is the English form of the name of the smallest letter in the Hebrew alphabet. Roughly corresponding in size and shape to an inverted comma in modern English script. The word "Tittle" indicates a little curl, or horn smaller in size than a comma, added at the corner or certain letters in the Hebrew alphabet to distinguish them from other letters very similar in shape. What Christ here says in effect is that the original text of the Hebrew scriptures is so accurate and authoritative that not even one portion of the scriptures smaller in size than a comma can be altered or removed. It is impossible to conceive how Christ could have more thoroughly endorsed the absolute accuracy and authority of the Old Testament scriptures.

Throughout his earthly teaching ministry, he maintained the same attitude toward the Old Testament scriptures. For instance, we read in Matthew 19:3-9, that when the Pharisees raised a question about marriage and divorce, Christ answered by referring them to the account of the creation given in the opening chapters of Genesis. He introduced his answer by the question, Matt. 19: 4, And he answered and said to them, "Have you not read that he who made them at the beginning made them male and female?" Notice once again that the phrase "at the beginning" constituted a direct reference to the book of Genesis.

Again, when the Sadducees raised the question about the resurrections from the dead, we read in Matt. 22:31-32, that Christ answered them by referring to the account of Moses at the burning bush given in the second book of the Pentateuch, the book of Exodus. As with the Pharisees, so with the Sadducees, Christ expressed his reply in the form of a question: Matt. 22: 31,32 "But concerning the resurrection of the dead, have you not read what was spoken to you by God, saying, V-32, I am the God of Abraham, and the God of Isaac, and the God of Jacob'? God is not the God of the dead but of the living." Christ here quotes from the book of Exodus 3:6, but in quoting these words recorded by Moses nearly fifteen centuries earlier, Christ said to the Sadducees of his own day, Matt. 22: 31, "Have you not read what was spoken to you by God?" In other words, Christ did not regard these writings of Moses as merely a historical document of the past, but rather as a living, up to date, authoritative message direct from God to the people of his own day. The passage of fifteen centuries had not deprived the record of Moses of its accuracy, or its authority.

Not only did Christ accept the absolute accuracy of the Old Testament scriptures in all his teaching, he also acknowledged their absolute authority and control over the whole course of his own earthly life. From his birth to his death and resurrection, there was one supreme controlling principle, which was expressed in the phrase, (That it might be fulfilled). That which was to be fulfilled was in every case of some relevant scripture of the Old Testament. By way of Illustration, we may mention the following incidents in the earthly life of Jesus, concerning each of which it was specifically recorded that they took place in fulfillment of Old Testament scriptures.

His birth of a virgin, his birth at Bethlehem, his flight into Egypt, his dwelling at Nazareth, his being anointed by the Holy Spirit, his ministry in Galilee, his healing of the sick, the rejection of his teaching and his miracles by the Jews, his use of parables, his being betrayed by a friend, his being forsaken by his disciples, his being hated without a cause, his being condemned with criminals, his garments being parted and divided by lot, his being offered vinegar for his thirst, his body being pierced without his bones being broken, his being buried in a rich man's tomb, his rising from the dead on the third day.

This list, which is by no means exhaustive, contains eighteen incidents in the earthly life of Jesus concerning every one of which is specifically recorded that they took place in order that the scriptures of the Old Testament might be fulfilled. It possible to say, without exaggeration or misrepresentation, that the entire earthly life of Jesus, from his birth to his resurrection, was controlled and directed in every aspect and in every stage by the absolute authority of the Old Testament scriptures.

When we set the fact side by side with his own unquestioning acceptance of the Old Testament scriptures in all his teaching, we are left with only one possible or logical conclusion. The old testament scriptures are absolute accurate. we shall now examine the practical effect which the Bible claims to produce in those who receive the word.

FAITH, THE NEW BIRTH, SPIRITUAL NOURISHMENT

Hebrew 4:12, we are told, "The word of God is living and powerful" or in modern English "The word of God is alive and active." The Greek work translated powerful or active, is the one form which we obtain the English word energetic. The picture conveyed to us here is one of intense, vibrant energy and activity.

John 6:63, Jesus himself says, "The words that I speak to you, they are spirit, and they are life." I Thessalonians 2:13, Paul writes to the Christians in Thessalonica, "For this reason we also thank God without ceasing, because, when you received the word of God which you heard from us, you welcomed it not as the word of men, but as it is in truth, the word of God which also effectually works also in you who believe."

We see that God's word cannot be reduced only to sounds in the air or marks on a sheet of paper. On the contrary, God's word is life, it is spirit, it is alive, it is active, it is energetic, it works effectively in those who believe it.

However, the Bible also makes it plain that the manner and the degree in which it works in any given instance is decided by the reaction of those who hear it. For this reason, James 1:21, says, "Wherefore lay aside all filthiness and overflow of wickedness, and receive with meekness the implanted word, which is able to save your souls." Notice that before the word of God can be received into the soul without saving effect, there are certain things which must be laid aside. The two things which James here specifies are filthiness and wickedness.

Wickedness denotes a perverse delight in that which is licentious and impure. This attitude closes the mind and heart against the saving influence of God's word. On the other hand, the word wickedness particularly suggests the bad behavior of a child. One occasion especially on which we call a child naughty is when it refuses to accept instruction or correction from its senior but argues and answers back. This attitude is often found in the unregenerate soul towards God. It is referred to by Paul in Romans 9:20, where he says, "But indeed, O man, who are you to reply against God?" It is referred to also in Job 40:2, where the lord answered Job and said "Shall the one who contends with the almighty correct him? He who rebukes God, let him answer it." This attitude, like that of filthiness, closes the heart and mind to the beneficial effects of God's word.

On the other hand, the opposite of filthiness and wickedness is described by James as meekness. Meekness carries with it the ideas of questions, humility, sincerity, patience, openness of heart and mind. These characteristics are in turn often associated with what the Bible calls (The fear of the lord). That is an attitude of reverence and respect towards God. We read in Psalms 25: 8, 9. 12, 14, the following description of the man who is to receive benefit and blessing from the instruction of God through his word.

Psa. 25: 8,9,12,14, "Good and upright is the lord; Therefore, he teaches sinners in the way. V-9, The humble he guides in justice and the humble he teaches his way. V-12, Who is the man that fears the lord? Him he will teach in the way he chose. V-14, The secret of the lord is with those who fear him, and he will show them his covenant."

We see here that humbleness and the fear of the lord are the two attitude which are necessary in those who desire to receive instruction and blessing from God through his word. These two attitudes are the opposites of those which James describes as filthiness and wickedness.

We find that God's word can produce quite different effect in different people, and that these effects are decided by the reactions of those who hear it. For this reason, we read in Heb. 4: 12, For the word of God is living and powerful, and sharper than any two-edged sword, piercing even to the division of soul and spirit, and of joints and marrow, and is a discerner of the thoughts and intents of the heart. In other words, God's word brings out into the open the inward nature and character of those who hear it and distinguishes between the different types of hearers.

Paul describes the dividing and revealing character of the gospel in 1 Cor. 1: 18, "For the message of the cross is foolishness to those who are perishing, but to us who are being saved it is the power of God." There is no difference in the message preached, the message is the same to all men. The difference lies in the reaction of those who hear it. For those who react in one way, the message appears to be foolishness, for those who react in the opposite way, the message becomes the saving power of God in their lives.

This leads us to another fact about the word of God in Heb. 4: 12, For the word of God is living and powerful, and shaper than any two edged sword, piercing even to the division of soul and spirit, and of joints and marrow, and is a discerner of the thoughts and intents of the heart not only is it a discerner, or revealer, of the thoughts and intents of the heart. It divides all those who hear into two classes, those who reject and call it foolishness, and those who receive and find it in the saving power of God.

Christ said, in Matt. 10: 34, 35, "Do not think that I came to bring peace on earth. I did not come to bring peace but a sword. V-35, For I have come to set a man against his father, a daughter against her mother, and a daughter- in- law against her mother- in- law." The sword which Christ came to send upon earth is that which John saw. In Rev. 1: 16, He had in his right hand seven stars, out of his mouth went a sharp two-edged sword, and his countenance was like the sun shining in its strength. Proceeding out of Christ's mouth was the sharp two-edged sword of God's word. This sword, as it goes forth through the earth, divides between members of the same household, dividing the closest of earthly bonds, according to how each member of the household reacts toward it.

Turing now to those who receive God's word with meekness and sincerity, with openness of heart and mind, let us examine in order the effects which it produces.

The first of these effects is faith. This is stated in Romans 10:17, "So then faith come by hearing, and hearing by the word of God."

Notice that there are three successive stages in the spiritual process here described. First, God's word. Secondly, hearing, third, faith. God's word does not immediately produce faith, but only hearing. Hearing may be described as an attitude of interest and attention, a sincere desire to receive and understand the message presented. Then out of hearing faith is develops. It is most important to see that the hearing of God's word initiates a process in the soul, out of which faith develops, and that this process requires a period of time. This explains why there is so little faith to be found among so many professing Christians today. The reason is that they never devote enough time to the hearing of God's word to allow it to produce in them any substantial proportion of faith. If they ever devote any time at all to private devotions and the study of God's word, the whole thing is conducted in such a hurry that it is all over before faith has had time to develop. Those who wish to develop real personal faith within their soul must be prepared to devote ample time to the hearing of God's word.

As we study how faith is produced, we also come to understand much more clearly how scriptural faith should be defined. In general conversation, we use the word faith very freely. We speak of having faith in a doctor of faith in a medicine or faith in a new paper or faith in a political party. In scriptural terms, however, the word faith must be much more defined. Since faith comes only from hearing God's word, faith is always directly related to God's word. Scriptural faith does not consist in believing anything that we ourselves may wish or please. Scriptural faith may be defined as believing that God means what he has said in his word. And believing that God will do what he has promised in his word to do.

For example, we see that David exercised this scriptural kind of faith in I chronicles 17:23, when he said to the Lord, "And now, O lord, the word which you have spoken concerning your servant and concerning his house let it be established forever, and do as you have said," Scriptural faith is expressed in those five short words, "Do as you have said."

Likewise, the virgin Mary exercised the same kind of scriptural faith, when the angel Gabriel brought her a message of promise from God, and she replied, in Luke 1: 38, "Let it be to me accordingly to your word." That is the secret of scriptural faith, "According to your word." Scriptural faith is produced within the soul by the hearing of God's word, and then is expressed by the active response of claiming the fulfilment of that which God has said.

We have emphasized that faith is the first effect produced in the soul by God's word, because faith of this kind is basic. To any positive transaction between God and any human soul. This is expressed in Hebrews 11:6, "But without faith it is impossible to please him, for he who comes to God must believe that he is, and that he is a rewarder of those that diligently seek him." He that come to God must believe. We see that faith is the first and indispensable response of the human soul in its approach to God.

After faith, the next great effect produced by God's word within the soul is that spiritual experience which is called in scripture the new birth or being born again.

James 1: 18, says "Of his own will he brought us forth by the word of truth, that we might be a kind of first fruit of his creatures." The born-again Christian possesses a new kind of spiritual life within him by the word of God received by faith in his soul.

1 Peter 1:23, describes Christians as "Have been born again, not of corruptible seed, but of incorruptible, through the word of God, which lives and abides forever." It is a principle, both in nature and in scripture, that the type of seed determines the type of life which is produced from the seed. A seed of corn, produces cord, a seed of barely produces barley, an orange seed produces an orange. So, it is also in the new birth. The seed is the divine, eternal word of God. The life which this seed produces, when received by faith to the heart of the believer, it is divine, incorruptible, eternal, it is the very life of God coming to a human soul through his word, for this reason the apostle John writes in 1 John 3: 9, "Whoever has been born of God does not sin, for his seed remains in him, and he cannot sin, because he has been born of God." The apostle John here relates the victorious life of the overcomer Christian to the nature of the seed which produced that life within him, God's own seed, the incorruptible seed of God's word. Because the seed is incorruptible, the life which it produces is also incorruptible, pure and holy.

However, it is necessary to warn that this scripture does not assert that a Christian can never commit sin, within ever Christian, a completely new nature has come. This new nature is called by Paul, in Eph. 4: 22-24, That you put off, concerning your former conduct, the old man which grows corrupt according to the deceitful lusts, V-23, and be renewed in the spirit of your mind, V-24, and that you put on the new man which was created according to God, in true righteousness and holiness. There is a complete and total contrast between these two, the new man is righteous and holy, the old man is deprived and corrupt. The new man being born of God, cannot commit sin, the old man being the product of man's rebellion and fall, cannot help committing sin.

The true Christian, who has been born again of the incorruptible seed of God's word, has with in him the possibility of leading a life of complete victory over sin. The unregenerate man, who has never been born again, has no alternative but to commit sin. He is the slave of his own corrupt, fallen nature.

The same is true in the spiritual realm. When a person is born again, the new spiritual nature produced with in that person immediately required spiritual nourishment to maintain life and to promote growth. God's word is so rich that it contains nourishment to every stage of spiritual development. God's provision for the first stages of spiritual growth is described in 1 Pet. 2: 1,2, Therefore, laying aside all malice, all deceit, hypocrisy, envy, and all evil speaking. V-2, As newborn babes, desire the pure milk of the word, that you may grow thereby. We see here that for newborn spiritual babes in Christ, God's appointed nourishment is the pure milk of his own word, and that this milk is a necessary condition of continued life and growth. However, it is not the will of God that Christians continue in spiritual infancy too long, as they begin to grow up, God's word offers more substantial food.

Consequently, they were still spiritually immature and unable to help others who stood in need of spiritual teaching. Heb. 5: 12-14, says, "For though by this time you need to be teachers, you need someone to teaches you again in the first principles of the oracles of God,

And you come to need milk and not solid food. V-13, For everyone who partakers only of milk is unskilled in the word of righteousness, for he is a babe. V-14, But solid food belongs to those who are of full age, that is, those who by reason of use have their senses exercised to discern both good and evil.

Christians who wish to mature spiritually must learn to study the whole Bible, not just a few of the more familiar portions. Beyond milk and bread, God's word also provides strong meat.

Again in Heb. 5: 13-14, "For everyone who partakes only of milk is unskillful in the word of righteousness, for he is a babe. V-14, But solid food belongs to those who are of full age, that is, those who by reason of use have their senses exercised to discern both good and evil."

What a picture of a great mass of professing Christians and church members today! They have owned a Bible and attended church for many years. Still how little they know of what the Bible teaches! How weak and immature they are in their own spiritual experience, how unable to counsel a sinner or instruct a new convert! After so many years, still spiritual babes, unable to digest any kind of teaching that goes beyond milk! However, it is not necessary to remain in this condition. Herbaceous tells us the remedy. It is to have our senses exercised by reasons of use, that is, to develop our spiritual faculties by regular, studying of God's word.

For this reason, the apostle John writes in his first epistle, Chapter 3, verse 9, "Whoever has been born of God does not commit sin, for his seed remains in him, and he cannot sin because he has been born of God."

The apostle John here directly relates the victorious life of the overcoming Christian to the nature of the seen which produced that life within him, that is, God's own seed, the incorruptible see of God's word. Because the seed is incorruptible, the life which it produces is also incorruptible, that is absolute pure and holy.

However, it is necessary to warn that this scripture does not assert that a born-again Christian can never commit sin. Within every born-again Christian, a completely new nature has come. This new nature is called by Paul, in Ephesians 4:22-24, That you put off, concerning your former conduct, the old man which grows corrupt according to the deceitful lusts, V-23, and be renewed in the spirit of your mind, V-24, and that you put on the new man which was created according to God, in true righteousness and holiness. The new man and it is contrasted with the old man that is the old, corrupt, depraved, fallen nature which dominates every person who has never been born again. There is a complete and total contrast between these two. The new man is righteous and holy, the old man is depraved and corrupt. The new man being born of God, cannot commit sin, the old man being the product of man's rebellion and fall, cannot help but committing sin.

The kind of life which any born again Christian leads is the outcome of the interplay within him of these two natures. The new man and the old man. So long as the old man is kept in subjection and the new man exercises his proper control, there is righteousness, victory and peace. But whenever the old man is himself and regain his control, then the inevitable consequence is failure, defeat, and sin.

We sum up the contrast in this way, the true Christian, who has been born again of the incorruptible seed of God's word has within himself the possibility of leading a life of complete victory over sin. The unregenerate man, who has never been born again, has no alternative but to commit sin. He is inevitability the slave of his own corrupt, fallen nature.

We have said that the new birth through God's word produces within the soul a completely new nature, a completely new life. This leads us naturally to consider the next main effect which God's word produces. In every realm of life, there is one unchanging law, as soon as new life is born, the first and greatest need of the new life is suitable nourishment to sustain it. For example, when a human baby is born, that baby may be sound and healthy in every aspect, but unless it quickly receives the kind of nourishment its nature demands, it will waste away and die.

The same is true in the spiritual realm. When a person is born again, the new spiritual nature produced within that person immediately requires suitable spiritual nourishment, both to maintain life and to promote growth. The spiritual nourishment which God has provided for all his born-again children is found in his own word. God's word is so rich that it contains nourishment adapted to every stage of spiritual development.

God's provision for the first stages of spiritual growth is described in 1 Peter. chapter 1, about being born again of the incorruptible seed of God's word. 1 Peter 2: 1,2, He goes on to say "Wherefore, laying aside all malice, all deceit, hypocrisies, envies, and all evil speaking, V-2, as newborn babies, desire the pure milk of the word, that you may grow thereby." We see here that for newborn spiritual babes in Christ, God's appointed nourishment is the sincere or pure milk of his own word, and that is this milk is a necessary condition of continued life and growth.

However, there is a warning attached here. In the natural order, no matter how pure and fresh milk may be, it easily becomes contaminated and spoiled if it is brought into contact with anything that is sour and spoiled. This same is true spiritually. For newborn

Christians to receive proper nourishment from the pure milk of God's word, their hearts must first be thoroughly cleansed from all that is sour and spoiled. For this reason, the apostle Peter warns us in 1 Peter 2: 1, "Therefore, laying aside all malice, all deceit, hypocrisies, envies, and all evil speaking. These are the sour and spoiled elements of the old life which, if they are not purged from our hearts, will frustrate the beneficial effect of God's word within us and will never hinder spiritual health and growth.

However, it is not the will of God that Christians should continue in spiritual infancy too long. As they begin to grow up, God's word offers them more substantial food. In Matthew 4: 3,4, Now when the tempter came to him, he said, if you are the son of God, command that these stones become bread. V-4, But he answered and said, "It is written, man shall not live by bread alone, but every word that proceeds from the mouth of God." Christ here indicates that God's word is the spiritual counterpart of bread in man's natural diet. In other words, it is the main basic item of diet and source of strength.

It is significant that Christ said here with emphasis, in Matt. 4:4, "every word that proceeds out of the mouth of God." In other words, Christians who wish to mature spiritually must learn to study the whole Bible, not just a few of the more familiar scriptures.

Beyond milk and bread, God's word also provides strong meat. This is described in Hebrews 5:12-14, the writer of Hebrews here rebukes the Hebrew Christians of his day on the ground that they had been familiar for many years with the scriptures but had never learned to make any proper study or application of their teaching.

Physical Healing, Mental Illumination

God's word is so wonderful in its working that it provides not only spiritual health and strength for the soul, but also physical health and strength for the body.

For our first text in this Connection, let us turn to Psalm 107:17-20, Fools, because of their transgression, and because of their iniquities, were afflicted. V-18, Their soul abhorred all manner of food, and they draw near to the gates of death. V-19, Then they cried out to the lord in their trouble, and he save them out of their distresses. V-20, He sent his word and healed them and delivered them form their destructions.

The Psalmist here gives us a picture of men so desperately sick that they have lost all appetite for food, and they are lying right at death's door. In their extremity they cry unto the lord, and he sends them that which they cry for healing and deliverance. By what means does he send these? By nothing else but by his own word. For the Psalmist says in Psa. 107: 20, He sent his word, and healed them, and delivered them from their destructions. We see, therefore, that both healing and deliverance are sent to use through God's word.

Side by side with the passage in Psalm 107 we may set the passage in Isaiah 55:11, where God says, "So shall my word be that goes forth from my mouth, it shall not return to me void, but it shall accomplish what I please, and it shall prosper in the thing for which I sent it." In Psalm 107:20, we read that God sent his word to heal and to deliver, and in Isaiah 55:11, God says that his word will accomplish and will prosper in the thing for which he sent it. God absolutely guarantees to provide healing through his word.

This truth of physical healing through God's word is even more fully stated in the book of Proverbs 4:20-22, where God says, "My son, give attention to my words, incline your ear to my sayings, V-21, do not let them depart from your eyes, keep them in the midst of your heart. V-22, For they are life to those who find them, and health to all their flesh." What promise of physical healing could be more complete. Health to all their flesh? Every part of our entire physical frame is included in this phrase. There is nothing omitted. Furthermore, in the margin of the standard King James version, the alternative reading for health is medicine. The same Hebrew word includes both meaning, God has committed himself to providing complete physical healing and health.

Notice the introductory phrase at the beginning of verse 20, "My son." This indicates that God is here speaking to his own believing children. we read that a woman of Canaan came to Christ to plead for the healing of her daughter and that Christ replied to her request by saying in Matt. 15: 26, "It is not good to take the children's bread and throw it to the little dogs." By these words, Christ indicated that healing is (The children's bread). In other words, it is part of God's appointed daily portion for all his children. It is not a luxury for which they have make special pleas, and which may or may not be granted to them. No, it is their (bread). It is part of their basic appointed daily provision from their heavenly father. This agrees exactly with the passage which we have read in Proverbs, Chapter 4, where God's promise of perfect healing and health is addressed to one of God's believing children.

Notice also that here in Proverbs, Chapter 4, as in Psalm 107, the means by which God provides healing is through his own word, for he say in Prov.4: 20,22,"My son, give attention to my words, include your ear to my saying, V-22, for they are life to those who find them, and health to all their flesh." The divine life of God himself, is for every need of soul and body alike, is in his word and is freely given to those who receive his word by faith. This is one further example of the vital truth which we stressed earlier, that God himself is in his word, and that it is through his word that he comes into our lives.

As we consider the claim made here in Proverbs 4, verse 20-22, that Gods words are medicine for all our flesh, we might call these three verses God's great medicine bottle, containing a medicine guaranteed to cure all diseases. However, we must bear in mind that on the human level, when the doctor prescribes a medicine, he normally ensures that the directions for taking it are written clearly on the bottle, and he indicates thereby that no cure can be expected unless the medicine is taken regularly, according to the directions. The same is true with God's medicine here in Proverbs. The directions are on the bottle, and no cure is guaranteed if the directions are not followed.

What are these directions? They are foretold. First, Prov.4:20, "Attend to my words," Second, "Incline your ear." Third, Prov.4:21, "Let them not depart from your eyes." Fourth, "Keep them in the midst of your heart."

Let us analyze these directions a little closer. The first direction is, Prov.4:20, "Attend to my words." As we read God's word, we need to give it close and careful and careful attention. We need to focus our understanding upon it. We need to give it free, unhindered access to our whole inward being. So often we read God's word with divided attention. Half our mind is occupied with what we read. The other half is occupied with those things which Jesus called, "The cares of this life."

We read some verses, or perhaps even a chapter or two, but at the end we have scarcely and clear impression or recollection of that which we have read. Our attention has wandered. Taken in this way, God's word will not produce the effects which God intended. When reading the Bible, it is well to do what Jesus recommended when he spoke for prayer, that is, to inter our closet and shut the door. In other words, we must shut ourselves in with God and shut out the things of the world and of time.

The second direction on God's medicine bottle is, Prov.4:20, "Incline your ear." The inclined ear indicates humility. It is the opposite of being proud and stiff necked. We must be teachable. We must be willing to let God teach us. The Psalmist speaks of Israel's conduct as they wandered through the wilderness from Egypt to Canaan, and he brings this charge against them. Psa.78:41, "They limited the holy one of Israel." In other words, by their stubbornness and unbelief they set limits to what they would allow God to do for them. Many professing Christians do just the same today. They do not approach the Bible with an open mind or a teachable spirit. They are full of prejudices, very often instilled by the particular

denomination with which they are associated, and they are not willing to accept any revelation or teaching from the scriptures which goes beyond, or contrary to their own set of thoughts. Jesus charged the religious leaders of his day with this fault when he said in Matthew 15:6,9, " You have made the commandant of God of no-effect by your tradition, V-9, and in vain do they worship me, teaching for doctrines the commandments of men." The apostle Paul had been a prisoner of religious prejudices and traditions, but through the revelation of Christ on the Damascus road he had been set free from them. In Romans 3:4, It says, "Let God be true, but every man is a liar." If we wish to receive the full benefit of God's word, we must learn to take the same attitude.

The third direction on God's medicine bottle is, Prov.4:21, "Let them not depart from your eyes." Where the word "them" refers to God's words and sayings. We made bring out the meaning of this third direction by quoting a remark of the late evangelist, Smith Wigglesworth, who once said, the trouble with many Christians is that they have a spiritual squint, with one eye they are looking at the promises of the lord, and with the other eye they are looking in some other direction. In order to receive the benefits of physical healing promised in God's word. It is necessary to keep both eyes fixed on the Lord's promises, one mistake which many Christians make is to look away from God's promises to the case of some other Christian who has failed to receive healing. As they do this, their own faith wavers and they too fail to receive healing, for James 1: 6-8, But let him ask in faith, with no doubting, "for he who doubts is like a wave of the sea driven and tossed by the wind.

V-7, For let not that man suppose that he will receive anything from the lord, V-8, he is a double minded man is unstable in all his ways."

A helpful verse to remember in such a situation as this is Deuteronomy 29:29, "The secret things belong to the lord our God, but those things which are revealed belong to us and to our children forever, that we may do all the words of this law." The reason why some Christians fail to receive healing very often remains a secret, known only by God and not revealed to man. We do not need to be concerned with such secrets as this. Rather, we need to concern ourselves with those things which are revealed, that is, with the clear and definite statements and promises of God given to us in his word. Deut.29:29, The things that are revealed in God's word belong to us and to our children forever. They are our heritage as believers, they are our inalienable right. They belong to us (that we may do them,) that is, that we may act upon them in faith. When we do act upon them in this way, we prove them true in our experience.

The need of focused spiritual eyesight is referred to also by Christ himself. One remarkable feature of human eyesight is that although we have two separate eyes, we should focus them in such a way that we form one single image. The ability to focus is referred to by Christ in Matthew 6:22, where he says, "The lamp of the body is the eye, if therefore your eye is good, your whole body shall be full of light." Notice here that Christ speaks not about the soul, but about the body. If our spiritual eyesight is properly directed and focused, it admits the healing light and power of God not only into our soul, but also into our whole physical body.

In speaking about the various avenues by which a teacher can reach a child's understanding, modern educational psychology has coined the two phrases (The ear gate) and the (The eye gate.) In considering the directions on God's medicine bottle, we find that in this, as in many other respects, God anticipated the conclusions of the psychologists by many centuries. The first direction spoke of (attending) the second spoke of (The inclined ear,) the third spoke of the (focused eyes.) God's spiritual medicine is to be received, with careful attention both through (The ear gate) and through the (The eye gate.) The inward center of the human personality at which the two avenues of the ear gate and the eye gate converge, is called in the scripture "The heart." We find that the fourth directions on God's medicine bottle concerns the heart, Prov. 4:21, for it says, "Keep them in the midst of your heart."

Proverbs 4:23, further emphasizes the decisive influence of the heart in all human experience. For it says, "Keep your heart with all diligence, for out of it spring the issues of life." In other words, what is in our heart controls the whole course of our life and all that we experience. If we receive God's words with careful attention, if we admit them regularly through both the ear gate and eye gate, so that they occupy and control our heart. Then we find them to be exactly what God has promised both life to our soul, and health to all our flesh.

The words of Psalm 107:20, are still being fulfilled today. "He sends his word and healed them and delivered them from their destructions." Christians who testify today of the healing power of God's word can say as Christ himself said to Nicodemus, in John 3:11, "We speak what we know, and testify what we have seen."

We can also use, to those who need healing and deliverance, the gracious exhortation of Psalm 34:8, "O taste and see that the lord is good, blessed is the man who trusts in him." Taste this medicine of God's word for yourself! See how it works! If is not like so many earthly medicines, bitter and unpalatable. Nor does it work like so many modern drugs, bringing relief to one organ or the body, but causing a reaction which impairs some other organ. No God's word is altogether good, altogether beneficial. When received according to God's direction, it brings life and health to our whole being.

There is one more effect of God's word. This effect is in the realm of the mind. It is referred to in Psalm 119:130, "The entrance of your words gives light, it gives understanding to the simple." Notice these two effects, "light" and "understanding."

In the world today, education is probably more highly prized and more universally sought after than at any previous period in man's history. Nevertheless, secular education is not the same as light or understanding. Nor is it any substitute for them. Indeed, there is no substitute for light. Nothing in the whole universe can do what light does or take the place of light. So, it is with God's word in the human mind. Nothing else can do in the human mind. Nothing else can do in the human mind what God's word does, and nothing else can take the place of God's word.

Secular education is a good thing, but it can be misused. A highly educated mind is a fine instrument just like a sharp knife. But a knife can be misused. One man can take a sharp knife and use it to cut up food for his family. Another man may take an exactly similar knife and use it to kill a fellow human being.

So, it is with secular education, it is a wonderful thing, but it can be misused. Divorced from the illumination of God's word, it can become extremely dangerous. A nation or a civilization which concentrates on secular education, but gives no place for God's word, is simply forging instruments for its own destruction. The history in technique of nuclear fission is one among many historical examples of this fact.

God's word is light. God's word imparted to me the light of salvation, the assurance of sins forgiven, the consciousness of inward peace and eternal life.

Hebrew 4:12, "The word of God is living, and powerful (or energetic), sharper than any two-edged sword, piercing even to the division of soul and spirit, and of the joints and marrow and is a discerner of the thoughts and intents of the heart."

It will be seen that this confirms and sums up the conclusions which we have reached concerning God's word. It reaches right down into the spirit and soul, the heart and the mind, and even into the innermost core of our physical body. God's word, implanted as a seed in the heart, brings forth eternal life, it provides spiritual nourishment for the new life. Received into our bodies it produces perfect health and received into our minds it produces mental illumination and understanding.

VI. VICTORY OVER SIN AND SATAN

The applications of God's word in our lives, First, we have seen that the only foundation of all true Christian faith and experience is none other than Christ himself, Christ encountered, Christ revealed, Christ Acknowledged, and Christ Confessed.

Second, we have seen that once this foundation of Christ has been laid by personal experience in our lives, we build upon it by studying and applying the teachings of the Bible.

Because of the supreme importance of the Bible in the Christian faith, we have examined the claims which the Bible makes for itself as the word of God, and the authority which it claims to produce. We have seen that the ultimate authority behind all scripture, both old and new testament, is that of the holy spirit, the third person of the God head. This is so because although many different human instruments were used in different ways to make the Bible available to men, it was the holy spirit himself who worked in and through all those human instruments, and who was able to produce an absolutely accurate and authoritative revelation and message of God to them.

Turning to the practical effect which the Bible, as God's word, produces in those who receive and apply it. We have examined in order the following five main effects. First, faith, second, the new birth, third, complete spiritual nourishment, fourth, healing and health for our physical bodies, and fifth, illumination and understanding in our minds. The next effect which we shall consider is this victory over sin and Satan.

We have already remarked that probably no character in the old testament had a clearer vision than the Psalmist David of the authority and power of God's word. For an introduction to our present subject, victory over sin and Satan, we may turn once again to the words of David, found in Psalm 119:11, "Your word I have hidden in my heart, that I might not sin against you." The Hebrew word here translated (to hide) means, more exactly, "To store up as a treasure." David did not mention that he had stored up God's word in the safest place, reserved for things that he treasured most, that, he might have it always available for immediate use in every time of need.

In Psalm 17:4, David again gives expression to the keeping power of God's word, for he says, "Concerning the works of men, by the word of your lips I have kept away from the paths of the destroyer." Here is a word of direction concerning our participation in "The works of men." That is, in human activities and social intercourse. Some of these activities are safe, wholesome, acceptable to God. Others are dangerous to the soul and contain the hidden snares of many names in scripture for the devil. How are we to distinguish between those which are safe and wholesome, and those which are spiritually dangerous? The answer is, by the application of God's word.

One often hears questions asked such as this, is it right for a Christian to dance? To smoke? To gamble? And so on. The answer to all such questions as this must be decided by the application of God's word. 1 Corinthians 10:31, "Therefore whether you eat, or drink or whatever you do, do all to the glory of God." Colossians 3:17, "And whatever you do in word or deed, do all in the name of the lord Jesus, giving thanks to God the father through him."

I point out that these two passages of scripture contain two great principles, which are to decide and direct all that we do as Christians. First, we must do all things to the glory of God. Second, we must do all things in the name of the lord Jesus, giving thanks to God by him. Therefore, anything that we can do to the glory of God and in the name of the lord Jesus is good and acceptable. Anything that we cannot do to the glory of God and in the name of the lord Jesus is wrong and harmful.

Recent researchers of medical science have brought to light one very definite way in which many modern Christians like David of Old, have been kept from the paths of their destroyer by the application of God's word in relation to the use or abuse of their physical bodies. The scriptures teach very plainly that the body of the Christian, having been redeemed from the dominion of Satan, the destroyer, by the blood of Christ, is to be considered as a temple for the holy spirit to dwell in and is to be kept clean and holy on that account. For example, the apostle Paul says in 1 Corn. 3:16-17, "Do you not know you are the temple of God, and that the spirit of God dwells in you? V-17, If anyone defiles the temple of God, God will destroy him, for the temple of God is holy, which temple you are." Again, in 1 Corn. 6:19-20, "Or do you not know that your body is the temple of the holy spirit who is in you, whom you have from God, and you are not your own? V-20, For you were brought at a price, therefore glorify God in your body and in your spirit, which are God's." Again in 1 Thess. 4:3-4, Paul writes, "For this is the will of God, your sanctification, that each of you should know how to possess his own vessel,(that is, the earthen vessel of his physical body) in sanctification and honor."

Not only does God's word give victory over sin, it is also the divine appointed weapon that gives victory over Satan himself. In Ephesians 6:17, the apostle Paul commands, "Take the helmet of salvation, and the sword of the spirit, which is the word of God," God's word is the sword which the holy spirit uses in the Christian warfare. All other items of the Christian armor listed here in Ephesians 6, the girdle, the breastplate, the shoes, the shield, and the helmet are without exception primarily intended for defense. The only weapon of attach which the Christian has is the Spirit's sword, the word of God. This means that no matter how carefully or completely a Christian may be armed in all other respects, unless he possesses a thorough knowledge of God's word and to know how to apply it. He has no weapon of attack, no weapon with which he can attack Satan and the powers of darkness and put them to flight. In view of this, it is not surprising that Satan has always, throughout the whole history of the Christian church used every means and device within his power to keep Christians ignorant of the true nature, authority, and power of God's word.

In the use of God's word as the weapon with which to put Satan to flight, the lord Jesus Christ himself is the Christians supreme example. In Luke 4:1-13, we read how Jesus being full of the holy spirit returned from Joran, and was led by the spirit into the wilderness, being forty days tempted of the devil. Luke relates how Satan brought three main temptations against Jesus, and how Jesus in each case met and defeated Satan with the same weapon, the sword of God's written word. For in each case, Jesus began his answer with the phrase, "It is written," and then quoted directly from the scriptures.

It is significant to notice two different phrases which Luke uses in this account of Satan's Temptation of Christ and its consequences. Luke 4:1, we read "Then Jesus being filled with holy spirit, returned from the Jordan and was led by the spirit into the wilderness." But at the end of the temptations, in Luke 4:14, we read "Then Jesus returned in the power of the spirit to Galilee." Before his encounter with Satan, Jesus was already full of the Holy spirit. But it was only after Jesus had encountered and defeated Satan with the sword of God's word that he was able to commence his God appointed ministry in the power of the spirit. There is a distinction therefore between being full of the spirit and being able to minister in the power of the spirit. Jesus himself only enters into the second stage of ministering in the power of the spirit after he had first used the sword of God's word to defeat Satan's attempt to oppose him and to turn him aside from the exercise of the spirit empowered ministry.

This is a lesson which needs to be learned by many Christians today. Many Christians who have experienced a perfectly scriptural infilling of the holy spirit nevertheless never go on to serve God in the power of the spirit. The reason is that they have failed to follow the example of Christ. They have never learned to use the sword of God's word in such a way as to defeat Satan and repulse his opposition to the exercise of the ministry for which God gave them the holy spirit. It may safely be said that no person has a greater and more urgent need to study the word of God than the Christian who has newly been filled with the holy spirit. It sad, such Christians often seem to imagine that being filled with the spirit is somehow a substitute for his word, and no matter how thorough he may be armed at all other points. A soldier without his sword is in grave danger. So, it is with the Christian. No other form of spiritual equipment of experience is any substitute for a thorough knowledge of God's word and no matter how thorough he may be equipped in all other respects, a Christian without the sword of God's word is always in grave danger.

The early Christians of the aplastic age, though often simple and uneducated in other respects, certainly followed the example of their lord in learning to know and use God's word as a weapon of offence in the intense spiritual conflict brought upon them by their profession of faith in Christ. For example, in 1 John 2:14, John in his advanced years wrote to the young Christian men who had grown up under his instruction, "I have written to you, young men, because you are strong and the word of God abide in you and you have overcome the wicked one." The apostle John here makes three statements about these young men. First, they are strong, second, they have God's word abiding in them, third, they have overcome the wicked one (that is Satan). The second of these two statements are related to the first and the third as cause is related to effect. The reason why these young Christian men were strong and able to overcome Satan was they had God's word abiding in them. It was God's word abiding in them. It was God's word, within them, that gave them their spiritual strength.

We need to ask ourselves this question of how many of the young Christian people in our churches today can we say that they are strong and have overcome the devil? If we do not see many young Christian people today who manifest this kind of spiritual strength and victory over the devil, the reason is not in doubt. It is simply, the only source of such strength and victory is a thorough, abiding knowledge of God's word. Christian young people who are not thoroughly instructed in God's word can never be real and overcoming in their experience.

We are today in grave danger of underrating the spiritual capacity of young people and of treating them in a manner that is altogether too childish. There is even a tendency to create in young people today the impression that God has provided for them some special kind of Christianity with lesser demands and lower standards than those which God imposes upon adults. In this connection, Solomon made a very relevant and penetrating remark in Ecclesiastes 11:10, "Childhood and youth are vanity." In other words, childhood and youth are only fleeting external appearances, which in no way alter the abiding spiritual realities which concern all souls alike. The deep, abiding spiritual realities upon which Christianity is based are in no way affected by differences of either age or sex. Christianity is based upon such qualities and experiences of the soul as repentance. Faith, obedience's and qualities are the same for men and women, boys and girls alike.

It is sometimes suggested that the way to meet this need of thorough scriptural teaching for Christian young people is to send them to Bible colleges. However, this proposed remedy can be accepted only with two qualifications. First, it must be stated that there is an increasing tendency at present, even among professedly fundamentalist Bible colleges to devote less and less time to the actual study of the Bible and more and more time to other secular studies. In Colossians 2:8, the apostle Paul writes, "Beware lest anyone cheat you through philosophy and empty deceit, according to the tradition of men." In first Timothy 6:20-21, Paul warns Timothy, "O Timothy, Guard what was committed to your trust (that is, the truth of God's word), avoiding profane and idle babblings and contradictions of what is falsely called knowledge-V-21, by professing it some have strayed concerning the faith. These warnings need to be repeated today. In many cases, it is possible for a young person to complete a course, at a modern Bible college and yet to come away with a totally inadequate knowledge of the Bible's teachings and how to apply them in a practical way.

The second qualification we must make is that no Bible college course, however sound and thorough it may be, can ever exonerate the pastors of local churches from their duty to provide all the members of their congregations with regular, systematic training in God's word. The local church is the central point in the whole New Testament plan for scriptural instruction and no other institution can ever replace the local church function. The apostles and Christians of the new testament had no other institution forgiving scriptural instruction except the local church. They got the job done more thoroughly than we see it done in most places today. Other institutions such as Bible colleges may provide special instruction to supplement the work of teaching done in the local churches, but they can never take their place. The most desperate need of the great majority of local churches today is not more organization or better programs or more activities. It is simply this, through practical, regular instruction in the great basic truths of God's word and how to apply them in every aspect of Christian life. Only by this means can the church of Christ as a whole, rise up in strength, administer in Christ's name the victory of Calvary, and accomplish the task committed to her by her lord and master.

This is with the picture of a Victorious church at the close of this age, given us in Revelation 12:11, where we read, "And they (the Christians) overcame him (Satan) by the blood of the lamb and by the word of their testimony." Here are revealed the three elements of victory, the blood, the word, our testimony. The blood is the token and seal of Christ's finished work upon the cross and of all that this makes available to us of blessing and power and victory. Through the word, and through word alone, we come to know and understand all that Christ's blood has purchased for us. Finally, through testifying to that which the word reveals concerning the blood, we make Christ's victory over Satan real and effectual in our lives and experience.

In the victory over Satan, we see that the word occupies a central position. Without proper knowledge of the word, we cannot understand the true merits and power of Christ's blood and our testimony as Christians lacks real conviction and authority. The whole of God's program for his people centers around the knowledge of his word and the ability to apply it. Without this knowledge, the church finds herself today in the same condition as Israel in Hosea's 4:6, concerning who the lord declared, "My people are destroyed for lack of knowledge, because you have rejected knowledge, I will also reject you from being priest for me; Because you have forgotten the law of your God, I also will forget your children."

VII. CLEANSING AND SANCTIFICATION

The nature of the Bible, its authority and the effects which it produces, which build us up in the Christian faith. To those who receive it with the proper attitude of heart and mind. These effects are first, faith, second, the new birth, third, spiritual nourishment necessary for Christian growth and development. Fourth, healing and health for our physical bodies, fifth, illumination and understanding for our minds. Sixth, victory over sin and Satan.

The seventh great effect of God's word is that of cleansing and sanctification. They key verses for this particular operation of God's word is found in Ephesians 5:25-27, "Christ also loved the church and gave himself for her, V-26, that he might sanctify and cleanse her with the washing of water by the word, V-27, that he might present her to himself a glorious church, not having spot, or wrinkle, or any such thing, but that she should be holy and without blemish."

There are number of important points in this passage which deserve attention. Notice first, that the two processes of cleansing and sanctifying are here closely related. On the other hand, although these two processes are closely related, they are not identical. We may express the distinction between them in this way. That which is truly sanctified must be pure and clean but that which is pure and clean need not necessarily be in the fullest sense sanctified. In other words, it is possible to have purity, or cleanness without sanctification, but it is not possible to have sanctification without purity or cleanness. Thus, cleansing is an essential part of sanctification, but not the whole of it. Later we shall examine more closely the exact meaning of the word sanctification.

Turning again to Ephesians chapter 5: 25-27, we notice secondly, that the one purpose for which Christ redeemed the church was that he might sanctify and cleanse it.

Paul says, in Eph. 5:25,26, "Christ gave himself for the church that he might sanctify and cleanse it." The purpose of Christ's atoning death for the church, and for each individual Christian in particular, is not fulfilled until those who are redeemed by his death have gone through a further subsequent process of cleansing and sanctifying.

Paul makes it plain that only those Christians who have gone through this process of cleansing and sanctifying will be in the condition necessary for their final presentation to Christ as his bride and the condition which he specifies in Eph. 5: 27, "A glorious church, not having spot, or wrinkle, or any such thing, holy and without blemish."

The third point to notice in this passage in Ephesians is that the means which Christ uses to cleanse and sanctify the church is the washing of water by the word. It is God's word which is the means of sanctifying and cleansing and in this respect the operation of God's word is compared to the washing of pure water.

Even before Christ's atoning death upon the cross had been consummated, he had already assured his disciples of the cleansing power of his word which he had spoken to them. In John 15:3, he says, "You are already clean because of the word which I have spoken to you." We see, therefore, that the word of God is a great agent of spiritual cleansing, compared in its operation to the washing of pure water. Side by side with the word, we must always set the other great agent of spiritual cleansing referred to by the apostle John. 1 John 1:7, where he says, "But if we walk in the light, as he in in the light, we have fellowship with one another, and the blood of Jesus Christ his son cleanses us from all sin." Here John speaks of the cleansing power of Christ's blood shed upon the cross, to redeem us from sin.

In order to form a complete picture of God's provision for spiritual cleansing, we must always set these two great divine cleansing agent side by side, the blood of Christ shed upon the cross and the washing with water by his word. Neither is complete in its operation without the other. Christ redeemed us by hid blood in order that he might cleanse and sanctify us by his word.

In 1 John 5:6, the apostle John himself places these two great operations of Christ in the closest possible connection with each other. Speaking of Christ in 1 John 5:6, "This is he who came by water and blood, Jesus Christ, not only by the water, but by water and blood. And it is the spirit who bears witness, because the spirit is truth." John here declares that Christ is not only the great teacher, who came to teach God's truth to men, he is also the great savior who came to shed his blood to redeem men from their sin. In each case, it is the holy spirit who bears testimony to Christ's work, to the truth and authority of his word, and to the merits and power of his blood.

John here teaches us that we must never separate these two great aspects of Christ's work. We must never separate the teacher from the savior, not the savior from the teacher. It is not enough to accept Christ's teaching through the word without also accepting and experiencing the power of his blood to redeem and cleanse from sin. On the other hand, those who claim redemption through Christ's blood must go on to submit themselves to the regular, inward cleansing of his word. 1 John 5:6, "This is he who came by water and blood, Jesus Christ not only by water, but by water and blood."

There are passages concerning the ordinances of the old testament sacrifices which set forth, the close association between the cleansing by Christ's blood and the cleansing by his word. For instance, in the ordinances of the Tabernacle, Exodus 30:17-21, we read how God ordained that a laver of bronze, containing clean water was to be placed in close proximity to the sacrificial altar of bronze and was to be used regularly in conjunction with it.

Exodus 30; 17-21, Then the lord spoke to Moses, saying; V-18, "you shall also make a laver of bronze, with its base also of bronze, for washing, you shall put in between the tabernacle of meeting and the altar, and you shall put water in it. V-19, For Aaron and his sons shall wash their hands and their feet in water from it. V-20, When they go into the tabernacle of meeting, or when they come near to the alter to minister, to burn an offering made by fire to the lord, they shall wash with water, lest they die. V-21, So they shall wash their hands and their feet, lest they die. and it shall be a statute forever to them--to him and his descendants throughout their generations."

If we apply this picture to the new testament, we see that the sacrifice upon the bronze altar speaks of Christ's blood shed upon the cross for redemption from sin, while the water in the laver speaks of the regular spiritual cleansing which we can receive only through God's word. Each is essential to the eternal welfare of our souls. Like Aaron and his sons, we must regularly receive the benefits of both.

Having noted the process of cleansing through God's word, let us now go on to consider the process of sanctification.

First, we must consider briefly the meaning of this word (sanctification). This occurs in many English words, and always is an active process of doing or making something. For example, clarification, means make clear, rectification means make right or straight, purification, means make pure. The first part of the word (sanctification) is directly connected with the word saint. In fact, it is simply another way of writing the same word and saint in turn is simply an alternative way of translating the word which is more normally translated (holy). The simple literal meaning of sanctification is (making saintly) or (making holy).

When we consider what the new testament teaches about sanctification, we find that five agents are mentioned in. These five agents are the following. First, the spirit of God. Second, the word of God. Third, the altar. Fourth, the blood of Christ. Fifth, our faith.

Sanctification through the holy spirit is referred to by both Paul and Peter. 2 Thess. 2:13, Paul says to the Christians, "God from the beginning chosen you for salvation through sanctification of the spirit and belief in the truth."

1 Peter 1:2, Peter tells the Christians that they are "elect according to the foreknowledge of God the father, in sanctification of the spirit, for obedience and sprinkling of the blood of Jesus Christ."

Both Paul and Peter mention sanctification of or by the holy spirit as an element of Christian experience.

Sanctification through the word of God is referred to by Christ himself. John 17:17, Christ prays to the father for his disciples, "Sanctify them by your truth, your word is truth." Here we see that sanctification comes through the truth of God's word.

Sanctification through the altar is likewise referred to by Christ himself. Matthew 23:19, he says to the Pharisees, Fools and blind! for which is greater, the gift, or the altar that sanctifies the gift?" Here Christ endorses that which had already been taught, that the gift in which was offered in sacrifice to God was sanctified, made holy, set apart, by it being played upon God's altar. In the new testament, as we shall see, the nature of the gift and of the altar is changed, but the principle remains true that it is (The altar which sanctified the gift).

Sanctification through the blood of Christ is referred to in Hebrews 10:29. Here Paul considers the case of the apostate, the person who has known all the blessings of salvation and had deliberately and openly rejected the savior and concerning such a person he asks, Heb. 10:29, "Of how much worse punishment, do you suppose, will he be thought worthy who has trampled the Son of God underfoot, counted the blood of the covenant by which he was sanctified a common thing, and insulted the spirit of grace." This passage shows that the true believer who continues in the faith, is sanctified by the blood of new covenant which he has accepted that is by Christ's own blood.

Sanctification through faith is referred to by Christ himself, when he commission Paul to preach the gospel to the gentiles. Christ states that his purpose is commissioning and sending Paul as follows. Acts 26: 18 "To open their eyes in order to turn them from darkness to light, and form the power of Satan to God, that they may receive forgiveness of sins, and an inheritance among those who are sanctified by faith in me." Here we see that sanctification is through faith in Christ.

Summing up these passages which we have read, we arrive at this conclusion. Sanctification, according to the new testament is through five great means or agencies, the holy spirit, the truth of God's word, the altar of sacrifice, the blood of Christ, and faith in Christ.

The process which these facts reveal may be briefly outlined as follows. The holy spirit himself initiates the process of sanctification in the heart and the mind of each one who God has chosen in his eternal purposes. Through the truth of God's word, as it is received into the heart and mind, the holy spirit speaks, reveals the altar of sacrifice, separates the believer from all that holds him back from God, and draws him to place himself in surrender and consecration upon that altar. The believer is sanctified and set apart to God both by the contact with the altar and by the cleaning and purifying power of the blood that was shed upon the altar. However, the exact extent to which each of these four great sanctifying agents. The spirit, the word, the altar, and the blood accomplish their sanctifying work in each believer is decided by the fifth factor in the process. That is by the individual faith of each believer. In the work of sanctification, God does not violate the one great law which govern all his works of grace in each believer, the law of faith. The law which is stated in Matt. 8:13, "As you have believed, let it be done for you."

Let us now examine a little more closely the part played by God's word in this process of sanctification. First, we must note that there are two aspects to sanctification. One negative and one positive. The negative aspects consist in being separated from sin and the world and from all that is unclean and impure. The positive aspect consists in being made partaker of God's own holy nature.

In preaching, both on this and other related subjects, there is a general tendency to over emphasize the negative at the expense of the positive. As Christians, we tend to speak much more about the (do nots) in God's word that about the (do.) For example, in Eph. 5:18, And do not be drunk with wine, in which is dissipation; but be filled with the spirit. we usually lay much more stress upon the negative "Do not be drunk with wine," than we do upon the positive "Be filled with the spirit." However, this is an inaccurate and unsatisfactory way to present God's word.

With holiness, the scriptures make it plain that this is something much more than a negative attitude of abstaining from sin and uncleanness. For example, in Hebrews 12:10, we are told that God as a heavenly father, chastens us, his children "For our profit that we might be partakers of his holiness." Again in 1 Peter 1:15-16, we read, "But as he who called you is holy, you also be holy in all your conduct, V-16, because it is written, be holy, for I am holy." We see that holiness is a part of God's eternal, unchanging nature. God was holy before sin ever entered into the universe and God will still be holy when sin has once again been banished forever. We, as God's people, are to be partakers of this part of his eternal nature. Separation from sin, just like cleansing from sin, is a stage in this process, but it is not the whole process. The final, positive result which God desires in us goes beyond both cleansing and separation.

God's word plays its part both in the negative and in the positive aspects of sanctification. The negative aspect is referred to by Paul in Romans 12:1-2, where he says, "I beseech you therefore, brethren, by the mercies of God, that you present your bodies a living sacrifice, holy, acceptable to God, which is your reasonable service, V-2, and do not be conformed to this world but be transformed by the renewing of your mind that you may prove what is that good and acceptable and perfect will of God,"

There are four successive stages in this process which Paul here describes. The first stage is presenting our bodies as living sacrifices upon God's altar. We have already seen that the altar sanctifies that which is presented upon it. The second stage is being not conformed to the world, that is being separated from vanity and sin. The third stage is being transformed by the renewing of our minds. Learning to think entirely new terms and values. The fourth stage is getting to know God's will personally for our lives. This revelation of God's will only be granted to the renewed mind. The old, carnal, unrenewed mind can never get to know our understand God's perfect will.

It is here, in the renewing of the mind, that influence of God's word is felt. As we read, study, and meditate in God's word, it changes our whole way of thinking. It both cleanses us with its inward washing and it separates us from all that is unclean and ungodly. We learn to think about things to estimate them, to evaluate them. As God himself thinks about things. Learning to think differently of necessity, we also act differently. Our outward lives are changed in harmony with our new inward processes of thought. We are no longer conformed to the world, because we no longer think like the world. We are transformed by the changing and renewing of our minds.

However, not the be conformed to the world is negative. It is not a positive end. If we are not to be conformed to the world, what then are we do be conformed? The answer is plainly stated by Paul, in Romans 8:29, "For whom he (God) foreknow, he also predestined to be conformed to the image of his son, that he might be the first born among many brethren." Here is the true, positive end of sanctification. It is to be conformed to the image of Christ. It is not enough that we are not conformed to the world, that we do not think, and say, and do, the things that the world does. This is negative. Instead of all this, we must be conformed to Christ. We must think and say and do the things that Christ himself would do.

Paul describes the purely negative type of holiness and dismisses it as quite inadequate. In Colossians 2: 20-22, "Wherefore if you died with Christ from the basic principles of the world, why, as though living in the world, do you subject yourselves to regulations, V-21, do not touch, do not taste, do not handle, V-22, which all concern things which perish, with the using-according to the commandments and doctrines of man." True sanctification goes far beyond this barren, legalistic, negative, attitude. It is a positive conforming to the image of Christ himself, a positive partaking of God's own holiness.

This positive aspect of sanctification and the part played in it by God's word, are beautifully summed up by the apostle Peter, in 2 Peter 1:3-4, where he says, As his divine power has given to us all things that pertain to life and godliness, through the knowledge of him who called us by glory and virtue, V-4, by which have been given to us exceeding great and precious promises, that through these you might be partakers of the divine nature, having escaped the corruption that is in the world through lust."

There are three main points to notice here. First, God's power has already provided us with all that we need for life and godliness. The provision is already made. We do not need to ask God to give us more than he has already given. We only need to avail ourselves to the full of that in which God has already provided.

Second, this complete provision of God is given to us through 2 Pet. 1:4, "The exceeding great precious promises" of his word. The promises of God already contain with in them all that we shall ever need for life and godliness. All that remains for us now to do is to appropriate and to apply these promises by active, personal faith.

Third, the result of appropriating and applying God's promises is twofold, both positive and negative. Negatively, we escape the corruption that is in the world through lust. Positively, we are made partakers of the divine nature. Here is the complete process of sanctification that we have described, both the negative escape from the world's corruption and the positive partaking of God's own nature of God's own holiness.

The point of the greatest importance is to observe that all this both the negative and positive is made available to us through the promises of God's word. It is in measure as we appropriate and apply the promises of God's word that we experience true scriptural sanctification.

In the old testament, we read that Jacob once dreamed of a ladder reaching from earth to heaven. For the Christian in the new testament, the counterpart to that ladder is found in God's word. It is foot set on earth, but its head reaches heaven, the plane of God's own being. Each rung in that ladder is promise. As we lay hold by the hands and feet of faith upon the promises of God's word, we lift ourselves up by them out of the earthly realm and closer to the heavenly realm. Each promise of God's word, as we claim it, lifts us higher above earth's corruption and imparts to us a further measure of God's own nature.

Sanctification is by faith. But that faith is not negative or positive. The faith that truly sanctifies consists in a continual active appropriating and applying of the promises of God's word. It was for this reason that Jesus prayed to the father. John 17:17, "Sanctify them through your truth, your word is truth."

VIII THE WORKING OF GOD'S WORD

Our Mirror, Our Judge

We shall examine two more effects in which the Bible, God's word, works in the believer. The first of these ways is that the Bible provides us with a mirror of spiritual revelation. This operation, God's word is described in James 1:21-22," Therefore lay aside all filthiness and overflow of wickedness, and receive with meekness the implanted word, which is able to save your soul. V-22, But be doers of the word, and not hearers only, deceiving yourselves." James warned us that for God's word to produce it proper effects in us there are two basic conditions. First, we must receive it with meekness, that is, with the proper attitude of heart and mind. Second, we must be (doers of the word, and not hearers only). That is as we receive the teaching of God's word, we must immediately proceed to apply it in a practical way in our daily lives. If we fail to do this, James warns us that we shall be deceiving ourselves, that is, we shall be calling ourselves by such titles as Christians or disciples or Bible students, but we shall not be experiencing any of the practical blessings and benefits of which the Bible speaks. We might sum this up by saying that the Bible works practically in those who apply it practically.

After this warning, James continues in the next three verses. James 1: 23-25, "For if any be a hearer of the word, and not a doer, he is like a man observing his natural face in a mirror; V-24, for he observes himself, goes away, and immediately forgets what kind of man he was. V-25, But he who looks to the perfect law of liberty and continues in it and is not a forgetful hearer but a doer of the work, this one will be blessed in what he does".

James here compares the operation of God's word to a mirror. The only difference is that a normal material mirror shows us only what James calls our natural face, that is, our external, physical features and appearance. On the other hand, the mirror of God's word, as we look, it reveals not our external, physical features, but our inward spiritual nature and condition. It reveals to us those things about ourselves which no material mirrors and no work of only human wisdom can reveal things we can never come to know in any other way or through any other means. Someone has summed this up by saying, (Remember that while you are reading your Bible, your Bible is also reading you).

Yes, the Bible is a mirror of the soul but in this as in its other operations, the result which it produces in us depends to a large extent upon our reaction to it. In the natural order, when we look in a mirror, we normally do it with the intention of acting upon anything which the mirror may reveal to us. If we see that our hair is untidy, we brush it, if we see that our face is dirty, we wash it. To receive the benefits of the mirror of God's word, we must act in a similar way. If the mirror reveals a condition of spiritual uncleanness, we must without delay seek the cleansing which comes to us through the blood of Christ. If the mirror reveals some spiritual infection, we must consult the great physician of our souls, the one in Isa. 53:5, "Who for give all our iniquities, who heals all our diseases." Only by acting practically and without delay upon that which the mirror of God's word reveals to us, can we receive the forgiveness, the cleansing, the healing, and all other blessings which God has provided for us.

It is at this point that many people fail to make proper use of God's mirror, to their own great spiritual use of God's mirror. To their own great spiritual and eternal loss. Through the hearing or the reading of God's word and the moving of God's spirit, they come under conviction concerning those things in their hearts and lives which are unclean, harmful, and unpleasing to God. Looking into the mirror of God's word, they see their own spiritual condition just a God himself sees it. They realize their need is one of sorrow and remorse. They realize their need and their danger. It may be that they even go forward to the altar at some church, pray, and shed tears. But their reaction goes no further than this. There is no real effectual change in the way they live. Next day the impression begun to wear off. They begin to settle down in their old ways. Very soon they have forgotten what manner of men they were, they have forgotten the unpleasant truths which God's mirror so clearly and faithfully revealed to them. Unmoved they continue the way to hell and a lost eternity.

However, the mirror of God's word can reveal not only the unpleasant, but also the pleasant. It can reveal not only what we are in our own fallen condition without Christ, but also what we can become through faith in Christ. It can reveal not only the filthy rags of our righteousness which we can receive through faith in Christ. It can reveal not the corruption and the imperfections of (The old man) without Christ, but also the holiness and perfections of (the new man) in Christ. If when God's mirror first reveals to us the truth of our own sin and uncleanness, we immediately act upon this revelation, if we repent, if we believe and obey the gospel, then the next time we look into the mirror, we no longer see our own old sinful nature, but instead we see ourselves as God now sees us in Christ, forgiven, cleansed, justified, a new creation. We are made to understand that a miracle has taken place. The faithful mirror no longer reveals our sins or our failures. Rather, it reveals to us the truth of such passages where Paul describes the new creation in Christ. 2 Cor. 5:17,18, "Therefore, if anyone is in Christ, he is a new creature; old things have passed away, behold, all things have become new. Now all things are of God, who has reconciled us to himself through Christ Jesus, and has given us the ministry of reconciliation". Notice that not only are the old things passed away, and all things made new, but "All things are of God." In other words, God himself accepts responsibility of every feature and aspect of the new creation in Christ, as it is here revealed in his own mirror. There is nothing at all in it of man's ways or doings. The whole thing is of God himself.

In 2 Con. 5:21, Paul says, "For he made him who knew no sin to be sin for us, that we might become the righteous of God in him." Notice the completeness of the exchange. Christ was made sin with our sinfulness that we in turn might be made righteous with God's righteousness in him. What is God's righteousness? It is a righteousness without blemish and without spot, a righteousness which has never known sin. This is the righteousness which is by God imputed to us in Christ. We need to gaze long earnestly at this in God's mirror until we see ourselves as God sees us. We find the same revelation also in the old testament, in the song of Solomon 4:7, where Christ, the bride groom, speaks to the church, his bride and says, "You are all fair, my love, and there is no spot in you." Here the flawless mirror reveals a flawless righteousness, which is ours in Christ.

Paul lays emphasis upon the need for Christians to keep continually looking in the mirror of God's word. 2 Corinthians 3: 18, But we all, with unveiled face, beholding as in a mirror the glory of the lord, are being transformed into the same image from glory to glory, just as by the spirit of the lord. We see that Paul, like James, is referring to the mirror of God's word. He tells us that this mirror reveals to us who believe, that our sins have been forgiving in Christ, never to be remembered anymore, but in their place, it reveals the glory of the lord, which he is waiting to impart to us by faith, Paul emphasizes that it is while we look into the mirror and beholding the glory of the lord, that the spirit of God is able to work on us and to transform us into the very image of those glories which we behold. In this, as in so many other examples of scripture, we see that the spirit and the word of God are always ordained to work together in harmony. It is while we look in the mirror of the word of God that the spirit works on us and changes us to the likeness of what the mirror reveals.

In 2 Corinthians 4:17-18, Paul returns to the same theme, for his says, "For our light affliction, which is but for a moment, is working for us a far more exceeding and eternal weight of glory, V-18, while we do not look at the things which are seen, but at the things which are not seen: For the things which are seen are temporary, but the things which are not seen are eternal." Here Paul teaches that the faithful victorious enduring of temporary afflictions can produce in us, as believers, results of great and eternal glory, but here again he adds the same qualification as in the previous chapter. This working out of spiritual glory within us is only effective, 2 Cor. 4:18, "While we do not look at the things which are seen, but at the things which are not seen. For the things which are seen are temporary, but the things which are not seen are eternal." If we once take our eyes off the eternal things our afflictions no longer produce the same beneficial effects within us. It is in the mirror of God's word that we behold these eternal things. Therefore, it is in this mirror that we must continue steadfastly to look.

In Hebrews 11:27, we read the scriptures record of our Moses fled from Egypt and endured forty years of exile in the wilderness, "By faith he forsook Egypt, not fearing the wrath of the king, for he endured, as seeing him who is invisible."

It was Moses' version of the eternal, invisible God and savior of his people that gave him faith and courage to endure and triumph over all his afflictions. The same vision can give the same faith and the same courage to us today. Where shall we find this continuing vision of God in our daily needs and testing's? In the spiritual mirror which he has given us for the very purpose, that is, in the mirror of his own word. The secret both of transforming grace and victorious living lies here in the use that we make of God's mirror. While we use the mirror aright, God's spirit works out these effects in our lives.

It remains to speak of one final aspect of God's word as it affects our lives, and that is of God's word as if affects our lives, and that is off God's word as our judge. Throughout the entire Bible it is plainly stated that, by sovereign eternal right, the office of "Judge" belongs to God himself. This theme runs through the entire old testament. For instance, in Genesis 18:25, Abraham says to the lord, "Shall not the judge of all the earth do, right?" Again, in Judges 11:27, we read, "May the lord, the Judge, render judgment this day." And in Psalm 58:11, "Surely he is God who judges in the earth," and in Isaiah 33:22, "For the lord is our judge."

As we move on into the new testament and methods of God's judgement. In John 3:17, Christ says, "For God did not sent his son into the world to condemn the world, but that the world through him might be saved." Again, we read in 2 Peter 3:9, "The lord is not slack concerning his promise, as some count slackness, but is longsuffering to toward us, not willing that any should perish, but that all should come to repentance." God delights to administer mercy and salvation, but that he is reluctant to administer wrath and judgement.

This reluctance of God to administer judgement finds expression in the way in which, as the new testament reveals, God's judgement will ultimately be carried out. In the first instance, by sovereign eternal right, judgement belongs to God the father. This is plainly stated by the apostle Peter, in 1 Peter 1:17, where he speaks, "And if you call on the father, who without partiality judges according to each one's work." Here judgement of all men is plainly stated to be the office of God the father. However, in John, chapter 5, Christ reveals that the father has chosen in his sovereign wisdom to commit all judgment to the son. John 5:22-23, Christs says, "For the father judges no one, but has committed all judgment to the son, V-23, that all should honor the son, just as they honor the father. He who does not honor the Son does not honor the father who sent him" Again, in john 5: 26, 27, Christ says,

"Far as the father has life in himself, so he granted the son to have life in himself, V-27, and has given him authority to execute judgement also, because he is the son of man."

Here it is explicitly stated that the office of judgement has been transferred from the father to the son. Two reasons are given for this. First, because with the office of judge goes also the honor due to the judge, and in this way all men will be obliged to show the same honor toward God the son, as they would toward God the father. Second, because Christ is also the son of man, as well as the son of God, that is, he is of the human as well as of the divine nature and in his judgement he is able to make allowance from his own experience, for all the infirmities and temptations of human flesh.

However, such is the grace and the mercy of the divine nature in the son, as in the father, that Christ, too is unwilling to administer judgement. For this reason, he in turn has transferred the final authority of judgement from his own person to the word of God. This he himself plainly states in John 12:47,48, "And if anyone hears my words and does not believe, I do not judge him; for I did not come to judge the world, but to save the world. V-48, HE who rejects me, and does not receive my words, has that which judges him- the word that I have spoken will judge him in the last day." This shows plainly that the final authority of all judgement is vested in the word of God. This is the impartial, unchanging standard of judgement, to Christ has assured us there will be one and only one standard of judgement, the eternal, unchanging word of God. At this scene will be fulfilled the words of David in Psalm 119:160, "The entirety of your word is truth, and every one of your righteous judgements endures forever." Here will be unfolded, in their absolute completeness, every one of the righteous judgements of God's unchanging word.

If we can but see it, this revelation that all judgement will be according to God's word is a provision of God's grace and mercy, since it enables us in this present life, to anticipate God's judgement upon ourselves and to escape from it. For this reason, Paul says in 1 Corinthians 11:31, "For if we would judge ourselves, we should not be judged." How may we judge ourselves? By applying to every aspect and detail of our lives the judgements of God's word. If we do this, and then by repentance and faith accept God's provision of forgiveness and mercy, God himself will never bring judgement upon us. Christ himself makes this clear in John 5:24, "Most assuredly, I say to you, he that hears my word and believes in him who sent me has everlasting life, and shall not come into judgment, but has passed from death unto life." This assurance is repeated in Romans 8: 1, "There is therefore now no condemnation to those who are in Christ Jesus, who do not walk according to the flesh, but according to the spirit."

What must we do to escape God's condemnation? We must hear his word. In humility and repentance, we must accept everyone of righteous judgements, as applied to our lives. In faith, we must accept record that Christ took our condemnation and suffered our punishment. Accepting these truths of God's word, we are acquitted, we are justified, we pass out from under condemnation and death into pardon and everlasting life.

All this is through God's word will be our judge at the last day. Accepted and obeyed, it assures us already of perfect pardon and full salvation through a righteousness which is not ours, but the righteousness of God himself.

My hope is for everyone to receive salvation through a righteousness which is not ours, but the righteousness of God.

YOUR BROTHER IN CHRIST JESUS-- LARRY COLLINS

And I give God all the glory for the revelation of this book and I think him and love him.

About the Author

The author is Jesus Christ. Larry Collins is the pen, I am a disciple of Jesus Christ, at NEW LIFE TEMPLE MINISTRIES. Pastors, Jerry and Carolyn Hayes 401 s. south 12th avenue Paragould ark. 72450. Where I receive salvation by faith in Jesus Christ. So surely goodness and mercy shall follow me the rest of my life and I will live in the house of the lord forever.

Printed in the United States
By Bookmasters